VE

ion

Living Unbroken

A Divorce Recovery Workbook

AN INTERACTIVE
BIBLE STUDY

Includes Seven-Session
Video Series

Living Unbroken

A Divorce Recovery Workbook

Tracie Miles

DAVID C COOK

transforming lives together

LIVING UNBROKEN: A DIVORCE RECOVERY WORKBOOK
Published by David C Cook
4050 Lee Vance Drive
Colorado Springs, CO 80918 U.S.A.

Integrity Music Limited, a Division of David C Cook
Brighton, East Sussex BN1 2RE, England

The graphic circle C logo is a registered trademark of David C Cook.

ISBN 978-0-8307-8297-0
eISBN 978-0-8307-8298-7

© 2022 Tracie Miles
The author is represented by, and this book is published in association with, the literary
agency of WordServe Literary Group, Ltd., www.wordserveliterary.com.

The Team: Susan McPherson, Stephanie Bennett, Julie Cantrell, Judy Gillispie,
Kayla Fenstermaker, James Hershberger, Susan Murdock
Cover Design: Jon Middel
Cover Photo: Getty Images

Printed in the United States of America
First Edition 2022

1 2 3 4 5 6 7 8 9 10

111921

Contents

Session Six: Chapters 9 and 10

Session Seven: Finishing Well

A Note from Tracie

Dear sweet friend,

Just knowing you're reading *Living Unbroken* and have committed to participating in this study makes my heart a little heavy, only because I know all too well the immense suffering you're likely going through right now. I understand how it feels to have a freight train barreling through your life, spinning fragments of destruction in every direction. And I understand how the fears and other emotions can feel like an elephant on your chest, as if there's no hope for the future and all your dreams have been ripped out from under you.

I am so, so sorry for what you're enduring. I wish I could give you a hug, wipe your tears, and sit beside you, because sometimes there's nothing more important than knowing someone understands and cares. However, because I can't be with you personally, my prayer is that your study group will become your support system during this difficult season.

While I'm sad that you're navigating the pain of divorce or separation, knowing you are reading *Living Unbroken* and completing this study also makes my heart leap for joy. Why? Because in doing so, you are taking a wonderful step in your journey toward healing. And that's no small thing! When it feels too hard, as it sometimes will, just remember, God will be going before your every step, and we'll all be walking alongside you as your heart begins to mend.

God sees how you're hurting. He already has a plan for you, your family, and your future—and it is good.

Congratulations on being courageous enough to begin the process of reclaiming your life. By opening your heart and putting your trust in God, you can feel positive about the future He has already planned for you, even if it's not the future you once imagined.

Before you begin this study, consider four important principles that will help you get the most out of this program.

1. Pray

Ask God to give you the willpower to commit not only to reading each chapter of *Living Unbroken* but also to being fully aware of His presence with you as you take this healing journey. Some exercises may dig up difficult emotions, memories, or thoughts you've been trying to avoid. Pray that your faith will keep you moving forward through those challenging moments, especially when you feel you can't make it through another day.

2. Trust

Make a vow that you will trust God no matter what happens. It's not easy to trust Him when life is hard, problems seem never ending, and joy is absent, especially when our confidence, self-esteem, and maybe even our faith have been shattered. But remember, "with God all things are possible" (Matt. 19:26 ESV), even recovering from tragic, heartbreaking circumstances. Trust that He will provide what you need at each step along the way.

3. Act

In addition to attending the study group meetings (whether in person or virtually) and discussing the questions with other members, I encourage you to complete the suggested activities found at the end of each chapter in the book. These action steps are provided to help you break free from the pain and begin embracing life with restored faith and happiness.

4. Journal

A journal can become a safe, precious space where you and God can meet every day, especially in the tender moments when you need to feel held and heard. We've created this beautiful workbook to be a place for you to record your feelings and reflections as you process through this study. I encourage you to write in it each day. Or if you prefer to use a computer, create a new document and title it "My Healing Journal" or "My Journey to Happiness"—anything that keeps you writing your way back to wholeness.

Keep in mind that the more time and energy you invest in this journey, the more rewards you'll receive as a result. With courage, focus, and faith, you'll find yourself in a different place by the time you complete the *Living Unbroken* study.

Right now your heart is fragile. I get it. Just remember, God sees how you're hurting. He already has a plan for you, your family, and your future—and it is good.

I am praying for you. Your group leader and your group participants will be praying for you too, and soon they will become your biggest supporters. Take a deep breath, my friend. View this study not as an obligation but as an invitation to embark on your new life with confidence and enthusiasm. We can do this together. And in time, you're going to be okay—maybe even better than okay. Because you're no longer walking this journey alone.

Before You Begin

I imagine right now you feel like you're fighting a battle. A battle to stay afloat financially, emotionally, spiritually. A battle to keep getting back up despite being terribly wounded. A battle to keep your children's hearts together while you try to mend your own.

Maybe you feel like you're standing alone in the rubble of your life, not sure how to move past the ruin. Or maybe the battle is still going on and you feel threatened from every side, knocked down time and again, with fear invading your thoughts and stealing your peace. Maybe you're even wondering whether you can make it out alive.

I understand. When going through separation or divorce, we may feel as if we're at war with an ex-spouse, former friends, in-laws, lawyers, or court systems. Yet the worst battle can be the one happening within—a war against heartbreak, insecurities, and overwhelming fears. It's easy to lose the fight against negative thoughts or escalating emotions.

Yes, the battle of separation or divorce can be long and painful, but we *can* find victory if we invest the time, energy, and faith needed to get to the other side.

Hold tight to the new friends you make in your group.

What's Your Battle Plan?

A battle plan is defined as "the plan for accomplishing a goal or dealing with a problem or difficult situation."*

No matter what stage of the battle we're in, having an intentional strategy is crucial if we long to see victory on the other side. *Living Unbroken*, along with the workbook you're holding, will serve as your battle plan.

In these pages, you'll be challenged to dig deep emotionally, process thoroughly, and dream passionately, all in an effort to help you bring about a paradigm shift in your thinking. You deserve happiness, my friend, and that renewed feeling of joy really *is* within your reach. I promise.

My prayer is that the exercises, reflections, discussion questions, journaling prompts, and support from your group members will help you persevere through the internal and external battles you're facing.

But let's acknowledge the obvious. You may be feeling anxious about joining a room full of other people—possibly strangers—and talking about your painful journey, especially when your heart is full of strong emotions and confusing thoughts. Maybe anxiety is whispering in your ear, planting doubts about whether a group study is a good idea.

- *What if I can't stop crying?*
- *What if my story is more painful or embarrassing than someone else's?*
- *What if guilt and shame feel so overwhelming that I'm afraid to let other people know my story and all that happened?*
- *What if people judge me or I don't fit in?*
- *What if the sadness seems so suffocating that I'm afraid to commit to being in a social setting, much less hearing about other women's pain? I mean, how can I be a comfort to someone else when I'm barely dealing with my own suffering?*

---

* Dictionary.com, s.v. "battle plan," accessed July 27, 2021, www.dictionary.com/browse/battle-plan.

Do these deep-rooted fears sound familiar? They certainly do to me because I've been in your shoes. And, unfortunately, I let those fears prevent me from attending gatherings that could have been helpful in my healing process.

These insecurities can keep us isolated from those who would provide the encouragement and hope we desperately need. Instead of finding connections with people who spur us on in our quest for happiness and love, we hide behind a false wall of self-protection, wearing our invisible warrior's uniform. Yet the battle continues to rage within, my friend, and that cloak of self-protection will only heighten your loneliness while standing in the way of your recovery.

Don't let this happen to you.

The well-known statement from Franklin D. Roosevelt rings true in this situation: "The only thing we have to fear is fear itself."** Fear will keep you stuck where you are. But courage can help you take the first scary step into this safe group of loving women.

Hold tight to the new friends you make in your group, and don't be afraid to let them into your life. They'll stay within arm's reach to catch you when you start falling again, and in turn, you'll keep your arms outstretched to catch them.

I also know from firsthand experience that, at times, the church can become the last place you feel accepted. You may no longer feel comfortable attending your couples Sunday school class. Maybe you don't fit in with the singles group either because everyone there is younger or older than you or you're still having trouble with the reality of being single at all.

Perhaps your church friends simply don't understand the situation. Maybe they don't know what to say or whose side to take, so they have quietly backed away from your friendship, adding to your pain (even though they love you dearly).

Maybe you've felt judged, misunderstood, or even ridiculed by fellow believers, some who may have instructed you to forgive "seventy times seven" (as mentioned in Matthew 18:22), as if you haven't already forgiven more than they know.

** Franklin D. Roosevelt, "First Inaugural Address of Franklin D. Roosevelt," March 4, 1933, https://avalon.law.yale.edu/20th_century/froos1.asp.

You may have even been encouraged to stay in a broken or abusive marriage at all costs by church friends who insist, "God hates divorce."

Or, perhaps, after devoting your life to Christian service, you've been told that you can no longer serve the church as a single or divorced woman, even if the demise of the marriage was not your fault. You may have even been married to one of the leaders, leaving you without a church home, especially if the congregation supports your ex.

Of course, you may not have had a church home to begin with (whether by your choice or your ex's), and now you may be wondering if you'll ever be welcomed anywhere.

God loves and adores you unconditionally no matter your marital status.

In any case, hear this: Regardless of your circumstances, God does not hate you. We read in Malachi 2:16 that God hates divorce, but He does *not* hate divorced people. Instead, He hates divorce because He knows it brings suffering to His beloved children. God loves and adores you unconditionally no matter your marital status.

If you've experienced any of these situations, picture me giving you a hug right now. I know that rejection and ridicule hurt. Being misunderstood and misjudged is unfair and cruel, making this difficult journey even harder than it needs to be. Sadly, this shunning, judgment, or exclusion from the faith community, whether intentional or unintentional, happens far too often to women who need the love and support of believers more than ever before.

That is one of the main reasons I wrote *Living Unbroken* and this study. I hope this group will serve as your safe and welcoming place within the church community by bringing you into a room full of women who truly understand and care. I also pray this journey helps restore your confidence in yourself, your God, and your church.

You are worthy and loved, and you belong at church and in this study group. Don't let anyone's judgment or well-meaning advice keep you from believing the truth of God's Word. A lot of things have changed in your life, but what hasn't changed is that you are a precious, beloved child of God—loved so much that Jesus gave up His life for yours (see 1 John 3:16).

Are You Ready?

This study will take a commitment of time and emotional energy, but just like anything else, the more you put into it, the more you'll get out of it. If you're committed to putting in the effort, I promise you'll finish this *Living Unbroken* study with a new warrior's uniform—one made of the armor of God—and as a bonus you'll be gaining a new group of mighty soldiers, fellow sisters and friends, to hold your hand through every battle while helping you find your smile again.

Today's the day. It's time to take your life back and sprint into the *unbroken* future that God has ordained for you. Let's get started.

Note: For an additional resource to help with your healing journey, subscribe to Tracie's blog at www.traciemiles.com and receive a free downloadable Living Unbroken Battle Plan workbook.

How This Study Will Work

The *Living Unbroken* study consists of several key components, and each one will play a critical role in helping you find healing and wholeness. Below you'll find a brief description of the real-life stories you'll read from other women, an outline of the activities you'll be doing in your private quiet time, and an overview of how your group meetings will be structured.

Stories of Hope to Keep You Hanging On

When we're in the middle of any battle, it can be hard to believe we'll ever make it through. Even if we do manage to survive the attacks, we may wonder how God will ever heal our hearts and mend our emotional injuries. Yet the truth remains: healing, wholeness, and happiness will come. The next time you start to doubt that, just repeat to yourself, *This too shall pass*. Because the despair *will* pass. I promise.

In this study, you'll read the stories of women who have walked this painful path of separation and divorce to reclaim peace and happiness. Although they've risen from the ashes, it wasn't long ago that they were feeling as broken and afraid as you feel today. Now God is using their pain for a purpose—to help your heart heal.

I encourage you to read these stories and let them serve as a reminder that the day will come when you'll have a story of hope and healing to share too. In each session, space will be provided at the end of the women's stories for you to reflect and journal.

- In what ways did you connect with these stories?
- In your past?
- In your current situation?
- What would you like to apply moving forward?

We may wonder how God will ever heal our hearts and mend our emotional injuries.

Quiet Time Activities

Moving Forward: Often we wholeheartedly believe God will do what He says for others, but when it comes to us, we aren't so sure, especially when we're recovering from something as devastating and unfair as divorce. In each session, you'll be given quotes from one or more chapters in the book to tuck into your heart. These encouraging words are there to help you move forward when the pain becomes too heavy.

Prepare: In each session, you'll be given nuggets of Scripture. Rewrite these verses in your workbook and on note cards or sticky notes as visual reminders of God's love. Also, spend time in prayer asking God to illuminate the truth of each verse and help you see how His holy words are speaking into what you're currently going through.

Purge, Reflect, and Protect: Each session includes questions to help you connect what you believe in your head with what you feel in your heart. Then God's Word, not your emotions, will direct your recovery.

Journaling Prompts: In each session, you'll be given journaling prompts to help you write your thoughts, prayers, and feelings. Journaling is a crucial part of your healing journey. You can write freely as you feel led or use the prompts to help you get started.

For example:

Today I feel … *confused.*

But God's Word says … *God is not a God of confusion but of peace (1 Cor. 14:33* ESV*).*

Always remember to pray as you journal. If you don't know what to pray or your prayers begin to feel empty, refer to the Scripture from the Prepare section, ask God to guide you to a verse that will speak to your current struggles, or do an online search using a keyword you want to learn more about in Scripture.

Here's an example of praying using the Scripture quoted above*: God, I know this confusion I'm feeling is not from You because Your Word says You are a God of peace and are all-knowing. Please free my mind and give me Your peace, as well as clarity and guidance, to help me put confusion behind me.*

At the end of this workbook, you'll also find a list of thirty-three prompts to help you continue journaling and form a long-term habit of doing so. Be sure to hold on to this study guide as a treasured keepsake to record how far you've come and how God has stayed with you every step of the way.

Happiness Prompters, Healing Steps, and Caring for You Reminders: At the end of each chapter in *Living Unbroken*, you'll find three sections calling you to take action in your life. While some activities may seem easy, each one serves as an important stepping stone to help you move forward. Try to carry out each and every suggestion—the difficult ones, the simple ones, and even the ones that may not make much sense right now.

Reading Assignment: You'll be assigned chapters to read for each session. This will prepare you to journal in this workbook and participate in the group discussions. During the study, carve out time to read the assigned chapters as well as the real-life Hope to Keep You Hanging On stories.

What to Expect from Your Group Leader

While some women may be going through the workbook alone, I hope that most will be joining group discussion meetings. In the first gathering with your group (a.k.a. future friends!), your leader will help everyone get to know one another and create an atmosphere of inclusiveness, safety, and love. She will foster discussion and guide you in filling out your Heart Check table, which is explained in session 1.

In all other group meetings, your leader will follow the format below to help structure the gatherings and facilitate meaningful conversations about the study content.

Video Session: Your group will begin each session by watching a video relevant to the reading assignments. In these videos, I share vulnerably and openly about the content while offering additional insight, encouragement, and inspiration. A link to each video is provided within the session.

Connection Point: Your leader will initiate discussion about the video and invite everyone to share their thoughts.

Reading Recap: Your leader will spend a few minutes sharing a brief summary of the assigned chapters.

Discussion Questions: Your leader will ask questions to prompt discussion of the assigned readings. All information shared will be confidential and kept safely within your study group, and together you'll navigate ways to apply the key takeaways to your own life to help you move forward in your healing.

Session One

Getting to Know One Another

Prepping Yourself for the Journey

Friendship Check

During this first session with your group, your leader will provide ways for you to get to know your fellow sisters in Christ and maybe even do a few fun icebreakers. Don't worry. Even if your heart can't fathom having fun right now or if you're the kind of person who cringes at the term *icebreakers*, your group leader will have a special way of setting your heart at ease.

This is your place. You belong here in this study, and you are not going to regret it! Even if it feels a little awkward at first, don't give up. The reward will be beautiful.

Keep in mind, this journey to wholeness isn't going to happen just by reading a book but rather by putting what you read into action. Make space in your life not only for reading but also for praying, pondering, and answering the reflection questions.

During your group gatherings, you can voice as much or as little as you want to share with the other members. But in your personal workbook, the only eyes that will see your written words (and maybe the tearstains on the pages) are yours and your Savior's. This is your safe place, so don't hold back writing down how you think and feel, because doing so will only delay your healing journey.

This Week's Verse

Prepare your heart for the study by memorizing this verse:

> He heals the brokenhearted and bandages their wounds. (Ps. 147:3)

Watch the Session 1 Video

The video is available at **DavidCCook.org/access**, with access code **LivingUnbroken**.

Heart Check

In the back of this workbook you'll find a Heart Check table. This activity is to help you see tangible evidence of your progress from working through this study of *Living Unbroken*. Prompts will be listed on the left so you can rank how you feel about each issue. You can also add your own topics based on specific struggles you're facing.

Be sure to fill in your Heart Check table today as you begin this study. Rank each line item on a scale of 1 to 10 (with 1 being the worst and 10 being the best). At the end of the study, you'll revisit the Heart Check table and enter your ranking for each line item again. During your final meeting together, be prepared to discuss your answers and share your biggest areas of growth, improvement, and healing.

Reading Assignment

Introduction

Chapter 1: When Your World Is Shattered

Session Two

Introduction and Chapter 1

When Your World Is Shattered

Hope to Keep You Hanging On

Kelly W.

Several years ago, the Lord saved me from an abusive marriage. I was married to a man who ridiculed me for everything I did, including loving Jesus. Despite all that, I prayed for my husband; I refused to see what *was* because I knew what *could be* with God. But when I thought it couldn't get any worse, I learned of my husband's unfaithfulness and the sordid details of many things he'd said and done behind my back throughout our marriage.

I was beyond broken. I couldn't eat; I couldn't sleep. But what hurt most was knowing that the God I loved and adored had allowed this to happen.

God alone knows the exact remedy to soothe our shattered hearts. Following the divorce, I buried my head in His Word and spent more time on my knees those first eight months than in all previous years combined. Though I cried enough tears to fill an ocean, God proved He is trustworthy and blessed me with my very own Jubilee year, just like in Leviticus 25. Remarkably, it was the year I'd be turning fifty; God graciously took care of all my finances, restored injured familial relationships, and even gave me a home in the same neighborhood I'd lived in before the marriage. But wait—that's not even the best part.

When a dear friend's childcare for her newborn son fell through at the last minute, she asked for my help. Had my marriage not fallen apart, I would never have said yes. Oh, what a blessing I would have missed! Every day I got to hold that tiny baby boy in my arms and rock him to sleep as I poured my heart out to God through songs of worship. There were moments that God's presence was so close I could feel His breath on my neck as He whispered, *"Kelly, do you see how you are holding this baby? Do you feel how relaxed he is in your arms? Imagine this is you, resting upon My chest while I sing over you. Fix your eyes on Me until I have become your confidence; let go of all your worries, My child."*

Five years have passed, and I still cry when I look over my journal entries from that year. But the tears aren't from pain. Quite the opposite. They stem from the overwhelming presence of God that shows up in the lives of believers when we want Him more than we want anything else on this earth. In retrospect, there are no words to express how much I cherish this bittersweet season. When I think about the time spent snuggled up with Jesus, I realize how few people experience this kind of intimacy with Him because it often comes at high cost and sacrifice.

In Matthew 16, Jesus explains to His disciples, "If anyone would come after me, let him deny himself and take up his cross and follow me. For whoever would save his life will lose it, but whoever loses his life for my sake will find it" (vv. 24–25 ESV).

> God *will* use the hard things we live through for our good when we place them in His hands.

As I let go and yielded all my desires to Him, He poured out His love, demolishing my fears of abandonment and rejection. I rebuilt my life in Jesus.

Sweet friend, I pray you'll find hope in this promise—God *will* use the hard things we live through for our good when we place them in His hands. Had it not been for this tragic divorce, I'd still have termites in my foundation—a false sense of identity that was leading me to seek security in relationships and in the role of being someone's wife.

Today I unequivocally declare: I am a different person, a new person, a much better person, all because God held my hand and led me through the refining fire of adversity. And you know what? I'd do it again in a heartbeat because nothing in this world is better than intimacy with Jesus.

Angela G.

I came into a relationship thirteen years ago full of love and hope, and I became pregnant a year after we started dating. Over time, I began noticing red flags but completely ignored them. He repeatedly refused to marry me, saying I was not worthy. The mental, emotional, and verbal abuse started shortly after. We broke up a few times, but we always ended up getting back together. I thought it was God's will for us to be together and that I needed to do anything possible to make it work, especially because we shared a daughter together.

Fast-forward to March 2020. COVID-19 shut down schools, and soon my place of employment was shut down as well. I knew I was in big trouble. The abuse became unbearable as it escalated. I kept pleading with God for help and accusing Him of not showing me a way to get out of that situation. I lived away from all family and friends except for my children. My mom had died a few years earlier, and I felt so alone. I didn't have anyone to talk to, so I slowly began to submerge myself in depression and just waited to die. I would only get out of bed to cook and take a shower and then … back to bed.

I told God I was giving up because I didn't see a way out. There was no way to escape my mess when everything was shut down. Hopelessness had set in. I finally stopped complaining to God and instead asked Him to end my suffering.

I was at the end of my rope when my boyfriend and I had an escalated argument. Although I was advised to run to the police, I was scared because I didn't want to hurt him. But I felt like God said, *"Enough is enough,"* and put His foot down.

A judge removed my boyfriend from the home that same day, which was a blessing. Yet with no job and no child support coming in, I had no idea how I would take care of my bills and put food on the table. But God had everything under control. People began helping in various ways even though I never asked for anything. God provided everything we needed and didn't hold back.

> God has shown me He will do anything to make sure His plan for my life is fulfilled and will not allow anyone or anything to get between our relationship.

My favorite Bible verse is Philippians 1:6: "Being confident of this, that he who began a good work in you will carry it on to completion until the day of Christ Jesus" (NIV). I didn't think I had a purpose, because I felt unworthy of love or anything good in this world. But how could I not trust in His goodness when it is written throughout the Bible?

It's been almost a year since that long-term relationship ended, and I am the happiest I have ever been. I know this is just the beginning of God's divine plan for my life. He has shown me His great faithfulness and continues to keep showing how much He loves me. Because of my past, it's not easy to put my trust in anyone or anything. But God has shown me He will do anything to make sure His plan for my life is fulfilled and will not allow anyone or anything to get between our relationship.

I have completely put my trust in Him because I now know without a shadow of a doubt that He is holding me in the palm of His hand and will never let me go. Friend, if you are going through separation or divorce and God hasn't fixed the relationship, it is only because He has something better for you. I have been hurting too, and I can confidently tell you: put your trust and life in His hands.

When we surrender all to Him, we will begin to see miracles, which give Him the glory and keep us in awe, boasting about His goodness for the rest of our lives.

Journaling Prompts

In what ways did you connect with these stories?

In your past?

In your current situation?

What would you like to apply moving forward?

Your Quiet Time

Moving Forward

> God always has a purpose for what we're going through and can do beyond what we can imagine.

Prepare

Prepare your heart for the study by memorizing this verse for the week:

This hope is a strong and trustworthy anchor for our souls. (Heb. 6:19)

Watch the Session 2 Video

The video is available at **DavidCCook.org/access**, with access code **LivingUnbroken**.

Note: If you're progressing through this study individually rather than in a group setting, you should watch each session's video before answering the questions in the workbook.

Purge, Reflect, and Protect

Introduction

1. How has divorce been like a death in your life?

2. Do you believe grief is a necessary and natural part of the healing process?

3. What obstacles do you think you may face as you embark on your healing journey?

4. What do you hope to achieve through this *Living Unbroken* study?

Chapter 1

1. Has your self-talk included "I wish I'd ..." about something you think you could have done to change the outcome of your marriage? Going forward, turn it around and instead complete the sentence "I'm thankful that God ..." with an item from your "Provisions List." (See page 83 in *Living Unbroken*.)

2. Whom do you need to forgive and for what?

3. What steps will you take to do this?

4. Reflect on Psalm 40:2–3. How can you find your way out of depression?

Journaling Prompts

Throughout this study, I encourage you to write down your feelings in the journal space of this workbook. As you progress in your healing journey, record your thoughts and feelings, prayers, important Scripture, and evidence of God working in your life. Include the date next to each entry to keep record of your progress over time.

Start by completing these journaling prompts:

Today I feel …

But God's Word says …

Happiness Prompters, Healing Steps, and Caring for You Reminders

Read through the calls to action in *Living Unbroken* (see pages 43–44), and try to complete each of them before the next session.

Reading Assignment

Chapter 2: Accepting What Is, What Isn't, and Who You Are

Chapter 3: Your Fears Are No Match for God

Reflections from the Group

Session Three

Chapters 2 and 3

Accepting What Is, What Isn't, and Who You Are

Hope to Keep You Hanging On

Julie L.

They were all looking to me for guidance, protection, and help. I knew he had crossed a line and I needed help. I needed someone else, the police, to step in and protect us. I was terrified … I was strong … I was unsure … I was certain … My kids needed me, and it was my job to take care of us. *Us*, meaning the five of us. That was different. We had always been a family of six, but all that changed the moment the protective mother in me was challenged by the love of my life.

The day a verbally and mentally abusive person switches to physical abuse is a scary day, yet a clear and freeing day. It is easier to see and know that you need to step away when a person crosses a line of physically hurting someone you love, even if you also love the one causing the pain. My desire was to protect my kids *and* save my marriage. I found that I was not completely able to do either. So I put my focus on my kids, not only protecting them but helping them with the damage that had already been done in their lives. In order to do that, a separation needed to happen. This is when I learned about the importance of taking care of me—the analogy of a flight attendant on an airplane who says, "In case of an emergency, put on your own oxygen mask first before helping your little ones with theirs."

This idea of taking care of me so I could take care of them was a new concept. With this analogy, I could see how I would be no good to anyone if I didn't take care of me. Taking care of me began for the sole purpose of being there for my kids. I also learned about boundaries and how to use them in my life. As I did, it became clearer and clearer that the toxic marriage I was in was not good for me, my kids, or my husband. I struggled with the idea that divorce would be God's plan for my life, but I began to fully trust Him with whatever those plans were and leaned on the verse in 2 Corinthians 5:7, which says, "For we walk by faith, not by sight" (ESV).

I was also trusting the sweet words from many people God had surrounded me with, who could see so much clearer than I could. They all had the same interpretation: I was in an abusive relationship, and God had a plan for me that was good. I was consistently reminded of Jeremiah 29:11: "For I know the thoughts that I think toward you, says the LORD, thoughts of peace and not of evil, to give you a future and a hope" (NKJV).

> I tried to do everything in my power to save my marriage, but God was revealing to me who He is, who I am, and how little control I really have.

God was patient and faithful to me during my separation. I had to wrestle with the thoughts that I had failed, that my kids were now from a broken family, and that I might live the rest of my life so differently than I had planned and imagined. After five and a half years of separation from a marriage of twenty-nine years, I filed for divorce. I was waiting for a miracle, and it didn't come. I had been waiting for clear direction from God, but He had actually given it to me—several times.

I finally had to let go, allow God to step in, and release my husband to his Maker. This was rough for me. I fought it. I tried to do everything in my power to save my marriage, but God was revealing to me who He is, who I am, and how little control I really have. It wasn't until after I filed for divorce that God gave me peace—"the peace of God, which surpasses all understanding" (Phil. 4:7 ESV). I knew I was right in the middle of God's will for my life.

As I walk through my divorce, I still believe in marriage. I still believe God hates divorce. But I have come to realize God loves me more than He loves my marriage. And that is an incredible reality that I am hanging on to and discovering more and more about each day.

Michelle S.

"I want a divorce!" My husband's cold words pierced my heart. It felt as though a fragile, treasured cup was carelessly knocked out of my hands, shattering into a million shards.

Fear paralyzed me. I stood in disbelief, wondering if it was even possible to move through the fallout. I held desperately to the belief that our five children and twenty-five years of marriage were worth salvaging through the wreckage. But he had already made choices and plans that did not include me!

"'For I know the plans I have for you,' declares the LORD, 'plans to prosper you and not to harm you, plans to give you hope and a future'" (Jer. 29:11 NIV). This had long been a verse helping me navigate life's storms. Yet now I not only felt betrayed by my husband but also abandoned by God. I had more questions than answers and couldn't imagine how any of this could be part of God's plans for me.

Grief devastated me. People talk about getting through the stages of grief (denial, anger, bargaining, depression, and acceptance) as if they're things you complete on a checklist. Grief really feels more like relentless waves that can catch you off guard and make it hard to breathe. Even when you see it coming, the power of grief will touch areas of life you never imagined.

Accepting something I did not want or believe in will always be challenging for me.

Everything my husband and I had built together was torn apart and divided or forced to be shared … our family, friendships, holidays, and life celebrations with our children and later grandchildren would never be the same.

Grief was no stranger to me. Many of the years leading up to the divorce are a blur. In a five-year span, I lost a baby I never got to hold, delivered a healthy baby girl, and watched helplessly as cancer claimed both of my parents. I was going through the motions of life in a fog. My husband and children *all* needed and deserved my attention, but I felt empty.

Sometimes you need to step away to gain perspective; God knew this!

> I came to understand that acceptance did not mean I needed to approve what happened. Acceptance simply meant I had to let go of my plans and trust God had plans to prosper and not harm me.

Even before divorce blindsided me, an opportunity came for me to go on a mission trip to Haiti with our church. I knew I had to do something or the darkness of grief would consume me. By serving from a known place of pain and loss, I hoped to find meaning and eventually healing.

I did not expect to be the one who was served. People with nothing showed me what real gratitude, joy, and faith look like. Our mission team delivered clean water to slums built amid garbage dumps. Children danced and cheered over drops of water in their buckets. We brought bags of food to a tent city where people welcomed us into their tarp and scrap-metal homes. Their eyes filled with tears of joy over the simple bags of food, which they saw as proof that God had heard their prayers.

Indescribable peace washed over me. I realized there was nothing I'd ever face back home that could compare to the unimaginable living conditions I'd witnessed in Haiti. And yet I saw how their joy was not dependent on their circumstances. They celebrated glimpses of hope for the future and trusted God's plan.

This was a pivotal moment in restoring my own hope. I came to understand that acceptance did not mean I needed to approve what happened. Acceptance simply meant I had to let go of my plans and trust God had plans to prosper and not harm me.

God *is* at work in the details.

It turned out that the food I distributed in Haiti was actually packed at Feed My Starving Children (FMSC), a hunger relief organization located near my hometown!

Seeing the profound impact of a simple bag of food inspired me to volunteer, pack meals, and eventually get a job working with volunteer groups during their packing shifts. My work at FMSC continues to serve as a reminder of God's amazing provision and plans for a future beyond what I could ever imagine.

Journaling Prompts

In what ways did you connect with these stories?

In your past?

In your current situation?

What would you like to apply moving forward?

Your Quiet Time

Moving Forward

Accepting what was and letting go of what can't be releases our hearts to focus on what is.

Prepare

Prepare your heart for the study by memorizing this verse:

> You are worried and upset over all these details! There is only one thing worth being concerned about. (Luke 10:41–42)

Watch the Session 3 Video

The video is available at **DavidCCook.org/access**, with access code **LivingUnbroken**.

Purge, Reflect, and Protect

1. Reflect on the idea that "it's okay to not be okay right now." How can you give yourself grace as you continue to grieve?

2. What labels are you placing on yourself that don't line up with who Scripture says you are in Christ? Ask Jesus to speak into your heart and mind about who He says you are, reminding you of your value on earth and in heaven.

3. Reflect on Malachi 2:16. What do you think God's attitude is toward you? How does this differ from what you have been thinking about yourself?

4. What tangible steps can you take today to accept your new life and move forward?

Journaling Prompts

Today I feel …

But God's Word says …

Happiness Prompters, Healing Steps, and Caring for You Reminders

Read through the calls to action in *Living Unbroken* (see pages 58–59), and try to complete each of them before the next session.

Reflections from the Group

Chapter 3

Your Fears Are No Match for God

Hope to Keep You Hanging On

Lisa P.

Dear Beloved, I want you to know that I am very aware of your situation. I see everything that is happening and what is going to happen. The agony of knowing you cannot afford your dream house in the country, which you just built with your spouse, hurts Me as well. Just remember, a house does not give you eternal glory. Only I can do that. A house is merely a shell for you to live in; *I* am what you really need to dwell in. It may feel like a hopeless situation, looking at houses that are more than your budget can handle and need a lot of work. Stop worrying. I can handle this. Just keep looking: you will know; I'm about to show you. When it seems like there is nothing left, I will reveal it to you.

—God

I remember standing in the hall outside my pastor's office, telling him I needed to find a place to live, and soon. My divorce was in the final stages, and selling the house my kids and I were living in was part of the deal. The clock was ticking, and I didn't have a lot of time left. All the houses in town that were even close to my budget were all either sold or just not going to work. I really needed God to move, and quickly, before my children and I became homeless. Fear became all consuming.

There was this one house, though. I'd driven by it a few times, noticing the For Sale sign in the window. It was not in a place I thought I'd like to live. I'd asked a few people about this house, and they'd said the kitchen was tiny, it had a small yard, and it was probably too small for my family. But I had run out of options, leaving me no choice but to call about it.

God knew what I needed before I even did.

The following day I showed up to look at the house. A cute little two-story brick home, it sat on the corner of Main Street and was within my budget. Because it had been sitting on the market for more than six months, I offered less—way less—and it was countered to an amount I could still afford. I couldn't believe how God had saved this house for more than six months just for me. It was perfect and everything I wanted. You know what else? I love living on Main Street. I live two blocks from where I work, across the street from the high school (making it easy for my older kids to roll out of bed and walk to school), only two blocks from my church, and a short walk to the middle school where my other children attend.

I am blessed to work in my yard and have friends honk and wave at me when passing by. I am blessed to have a front-row seat to any parade in town. I am blessed to be able to walk or ride my bike to most locations. And when COVID-19 left us stuck at home indefinitely, the central location enabled us to see people, talk to neighbors, say hi to anyone walking by our house, wave to friends driving by, and just sit on the front porch watching the happenings around town.

God knew what I needed before I even did. He knew what was ahead of me, and our God is a God of miracles.

Natalie R.

As a child growing up and into my teen years, all I really wanted was to one day be a wife and mother. After college and beginning my career, I married my husband, who had graduated with a ministerial degree from a Bible college where we were living in California. A few years into our marriage, we welcomed our son, and four years later, our daughter joined the family. My thirties were a blur of raising children, family life, working as a court reporter, and all the ups and downs that church ministry had to offer.

At the age of forty, my life took a sharp turn in a direction I never thought it would go when I was given a breast cancer diagnosis. The next fifteen months were filled with numerous surgeries and recovery. It was shortly after that period of time that I really began to reflect on my life and all that had gone on in my marriage over the past few decades. Things were not okay, even as my husband had tried to convince me they were. We began to deal with the real issues in the marriage, which included addiction and infidelity on his part and a lot of passivity and enabling on my part. And although we fought for recovery and healing in our marriage for months and years, sadly it ended after almost twenty-five years of marriage.

To say I was broken is an understatement. My son was in college at the time, and my daughter a sophomore in high school … definitely not a good time for a divorce (really, there is no good time). At that point, I no longer had my career, was a breast cancer survivor, and had been out of the workforce for some time. I had no idea how I would make ends meet or even survive the devastation that was now my current reality. I knew I would need the Lord's help on a daily basis.

From those early days of my separation and divorce, I have countless stories of God's provision. There was the job that came by way of my dentist office calling me up and asking if I wanted to work for them. There was the darling VRBO rental that became a permanent home for my daughter and me as she completed high school. We still reminisce about the memories made in that little house that was our "safe haven." There was the time I ran completely out of money. I had automatic payments drafting from an account with a zero balance … ugh! But God provided for me through a dear friend who felt led to put ten $100 bills in a cute little coupon book she'd made and presented to me. The stories of God's provision are too numerous to count.

At the end of my long divorce process, I was left hurting and hopeless, certain that life would never be good again. I wondered if I'd be whole again, if I'd be single the rest of my life, if I'd ever retire or just work until the day I died. My mind swirled in so many different directions. In the midst of the confusion, I felt the Lord whispering to my heart, *"Do you trust that I know what is best for your life?"* And I sensed Him offering to take me by the hand and lead me through the next season, whatever that looked like.

> *It is possible to live again and blossom in the season of life that you find yourself in.*

It has not been easy. It has been a much slower process than I would have liked. I have made mistakes.

But in the midst of it all, God has been faithful to provide friendships and the support of other women. I have by no means "arrived," and my healing continues, but I'm here to tell you that it is possible to live again and blossom in the season of life that you find yourself in.

Romans 15:13 says, "May the God of hope fill you with all joy and peace as you trust in him" (NIV). I now want to reach out and help other women find hope in their journey, just as I have found hope in mine.

Journaling Prompts

In what ways did you connect with these stories?

In your past?

In your current situation?

What would you like to apply moving forward?

Your Quiet Time

Moving Forward

It's okay and normal to have fears, but it's not okay to let them have you.

Prepare

Prepare your heart for the study by memorizing this verse:

> Don't be afraid, for I am with you.
>
> > Don't be discouraged, for I am your God.
>
> I will strengthen you and help you.
>
> > I will hold you up with my victorious right hand. (Isa. 41:10)

Purge, Reflect, and Protect

1. What fears are weighing you down? Make a list, and release them to God by speaking them out loud in prayer.

2. How have you seen God's provision in your life? How does being aware that God is at work in your life, even in the worst of circumstances, give you hope that He will continue to provide for you in miraculous ways?

3. Reflect on Psalm 46:1–3 and Psalm 89:15–16. Which words resonate with you? Which words give you peace?

4. What are you going to do today to start taking back your happiness?

Journaling Prompts

Today I feel …

But God's Word says …

Happiness Prompters, Healing Steps, and Caring for You Reminders

Read through the calls to action in *Living Unbroken* (see pages 82–84), and try to complete each of them before the next session.

Reading Assignment

Chapter 4: Overcoming Loneliness

Chapter 5: Making the Most of Your Singleness

Reflections from the Group

Session Four

Chapters 4 and 5

Overcoming Loneliness

Hope to Keep You Hanging On

Kristi W.

I never stopped praying for reconciliation until our divorce was final. We were separated for nearly three years. Three. Hard. Years. One thing I was convicted about early on was that I was not responsible for his actions, but I was 100 percent accountable for my reactions.

Even in separation, he was still my husband, and as difficult as it was to show him respect, that was my biblical mandate. It was not easy, and I didn't do it perfectly, but one way I chose to respect him was to hold my tongue. Psalm 62:5–8 says,

> For God alone, O my soul, wait in silence,
>   for my hope is from him.
> He only is my rock and my salvation,
>   my fortress; I shall not be shaken.
> On God rests my salvation and my glory;
>   my mighty rock, my refuge is God.
> Trust in him at all times, O people;
>   pour out your heart before him;
>   God is a refuge for us. (ESV)

Believe me, I wanted to tell everyone how I had been wronged. I wanted sympathy and compassion because I was alone and wounded. I wanted others to know the whole sordid tale to help me feel vindicated. But as much as I wanted pity for my new circumstance, I wanted God to do a miracle and restore my marriage even more.

I made the choice to wait in silence and pour out my heart to God and a very, very small circle of friends. I chose them carefully. Two of them had unfaithful husbands, and the Lord in His goodness had restored their marriages. They gave me hope that God might work a miracle in my marriage too.

> *I was not responsible for his actions, but I was 100 percent accountable for my reactions.*

Another friend worked with me on a daily basis and saw more of my raw emotion than others did. I trusted her to keep my confidence. Another two friends lived in other states. It helped that they didn't know my husband and were there to support me without knowing all the details. This godly core of women kept me upright as I processed my loss and grief throughout my separation.

They helped me, prayed for me, and loved me. I believe I am a better friend today because of their example of friendship during that time. However, I was just as careful about who I *didn't* share with. My immediate family knew the circumstances of my separation, but I intentionally chose not to share the ups and downs of those years with them. They were my family, and I knew that they would welcome my husband back if he repented, but the more they knew, the harder it would be for them to move past their own feelings of betrayal.

Other friends I kept at arm's length and asked for different things from them. I needed to just spend time laughing with one friend, an escape from the heaviness of my everyday existence. I didn't want to rehash the latest drama whenever we got together. I chose to attend a new church and intentionally didn't get plugged in right away so my husband wouldn't feel awkward if he ever wanted to come with me. My goal was not to shame my husband. I did this by keeping my mouth shut and my circle close. I never wanted him to have an excuse for not reconciling because I had shared personal details with everyone who would listen.

Perhaps most importantly, throughout that whole time, I learned how to pour out my heart to the Lord. I read through the Bible for the first time in my life and learned to pray Scripture. I wrote verses that spoke to me in my grief. I learned what it was to be comforted by the only One who could make me feel better. I realized that He was enough then and He's still enough five years after our divorce.

You don't need to take your show on the road, friend. Handpick your support team carefully. Hold your tongue as a way to honor the vow you took. Pour out your heart to the One who loves you more than you can comprehend, and He will cover you with His love!

Sandra A.

May 2014 is a month I will never forget—the month I found out my husband and the father to our then six-year-old son was cheating on me and was leaving us.

The pain that tore through me is something I had never experienced before and hope never to go through again, especially when my ex-mother-in-law served me with divorce papers on my birthday.

I never thought the pain would end. The betrayal, anguish, and anger were unceasing, as were the questions … so many questions. After the official end to my marriage, five years of praying and crying ensued as I dealt with all the anger and pain in my quest toward healing.

Looking back, although I did not see it at the time, during the first couple years God was working mightily to bring the most amazing godly people into my life, such as my brothers, sister-in-law, friends, and ladies from my church. They would cry with me, pray with me, let me vent, and give me Jesus, always pointing back to Jesus while pouring into me and my son.

I would receive so many verses that comforted my heart and would hear from the Lord about wonderful promises, but admittedly, I could not see God at work at the time. Instead, I would see the man I loved (and the one I'd thought I would spend the rest of my life with) look like he was "winning" and doing great, while I was the one suffering. It felt so unfair.

Anger always arose as I struggled with thoughts like *Why does he get to do these things? Why isn't God intervening? Why are my son and I the ones struggling and trying to survive when none of this was our fault?*

But somehow God gave me the strength daily to keep pushing forward, and 2 Corinthians 4:8–9 became true in my life: "We are pressed on every side by troubles, but we are not crushed. We are perplexed, but not driven to despair. We are hunted down, but never abandoned by God. We get knocked down, but we are not destroyed." Because of faith I was able to continue walking with God and showing His grace to others, including my husband.

Galatians 6:9 says, "So let's not get tired of doing what is good. At just the right time we will reap a harvest of blessing if we don't give up." This verse frequently came to mind as well but was the hardest verse to live out, especially with a person who was constantly hurting me and our son. It was so hard to sit in court across from someone I no longer recognized, and yet this verse is a promise I kept close to my heart. I held on to the belief that in due time we would reap the harvest.

Although I did not see it at the time, during the first couple years God was working mightily to bring the most amazing godly people into my life.

After five years, I gave up thinking I would ever reap any rewards from all the good I'd done. I stopped praying for the man who was no longer my husband, a man who now belonged to someone else. Isaiah 43:19 would often come to mind or be part of my Bible reading: "For I am about to do something new. See, I have already begun! Do you not see it? I will make a pathway through the wilderness. I will create rivers in the dry wasteland."

Over and over, I would read this verse, and at one point I even threw the Bible and screamed at God: "No! I don't see it! Nothing is new. Everything is dead and over. I am tired of Your promises. Where were You when he was doing the things he was doing? Where were You when I thought I was marrying a godly man? I did everything right! Why, God? Just why?"

Because God is so good, and despite my emotions, I felt His presence wrap around me as I wailed. In time, I received a letter from my ex-husband sincerely apologizing for who he had become and how he had walked away from the Lord and our family. Sharing that he saw Jesus in me and in our son, he has returned to the Lord. Today I am friends with my ex-husband's new wife, who has also relied on me as a mentor. "I am doing a new thing; now it springs forth, do you not perceive it?" (Isa. 43:19 ESV).

Now I see.

I am nearing completion of my degree to become a child and adolescent counselor, and our son, who is about to be thirteen, loves Jesus deeply due to having to rely on Him through his hurt. *I am doing a new thing …*"

In our darkest times, God is there. He is moving and working, even when we don't see it. Do not give up. Cry out to God and allow Him to heal you. God isn't afraid of our emotions, and we shouldn't be either. Give it all to God, and allow Him to heal you from the inside out. It will happen.

Journaling Prompts

In what ways did you connect with these stories?

In your past?

In your current situation?

What would you like to apply moving forward?

Your Quiet Time

Moving Forward

> *Whether we are married, divorced, or single, God is the One who is always by our side.*

Prepare

Prepare your heart for the study by memorizing this verse:

> This is my command—be strong and courageous! Do not be afraid or discouraged. For the LORD your God is with you wherever you go. (Josh. 1:9)

Watch the Session 4 Video

The video is available at **DavidCCook.org/access**, with access code **LivingUnbroken**.

Purge, Reflect, and Protect

1. How are you handling your increased alone time? Have you ever heard God whisper, *"You're going to make it"*? Ask God for an increased awareness of His presence and strength to help you seek healthy and creative ways to fill your spare time.

2. Do you relate to any of the faces of loneliness? Which ones and why?

3. What ideas did this chapter give you about positive ways to fight the battle against loneliness?

4. Reflect on Psalm 139. Which words help you feel less alone?

Journaling Prompts

Today I feel …

But God's Word says …

Happiness Prompters, Healing Steps, and Caring for You Reminders

Read through the calls to action in *Living Unbroken* (see pages 99–100), and try to complete each of them before the next session.

Reflections from the Group

Chapter 5

Making the Most of Your Singleness

Hope to Keep You Hanging On

Sharon G.

Teacher, mother, daughter, and sister. These are some of the labels I use to describe myself. But two years ago, I added a new one: divorced … again.

My first divorce was due to my husband's homosexuality. Honestly, this gave me a false sense of "it was him, not me." Reflecting back, this sense of faultlessness may have caused me to rush into my second marriage, and what a whirlwind romance it was. Until it wasn't. Even though we'd both made prideful choices that created a loveless marriage, he ultimately ended it. With little reason why, he chose not to reconcile, leaving me with unresolved hurt and feelings of worthlessness.

Divorce, unlike other love loss, happens because of someone's choice. It seemed like my husband had ended our marriage simply because of who I was. The years I was numb in our marriage were no protection from the heavy weight of sorrow that settled in. Moments from my past parked themselves in my memory. Emotional triggers were everywhere, and guilt, shame, and confusion became my new labels. My Christian counselor told me I had to walk through this pain. But I needed more than words of hope; I needed to know *how* to get to the other side. I started with this promise: "This means that anyone who belongs to Christ has become a new person. The old life is gone; a new life has begun!" (2 Cor. 5:17).

To become new, I had to take an honest look at who I was. Through prayer and honest conversations with my family, my greatest faults were revealed to me. I had to get a handle on my unrealistic expectations and mismanaged emotions. It was easy to talk about all the ways *I* had been wronged, but I had to acknowledge my part (see Ps. 139:23–24). I had already accepted Christ's unconditional love, so I had nothing to lose but my old self and the weight of my past.

Allowing God to transform me into someone new was the beginning of my healing; time continued to do the rest. I used to resent well-intentioned people telling me time would heal, yet this has proven to be true. I called on God to help me make this time intentional. I read books from Christian authors, joined Bible studies, and built friendships with other Christian women. I began serving at my local church, and I began writing.

I refuse to let divorce be the end of my story, and I have stopped letting the past define me.

I don't want to make it sound like I marched forward each day confidently. No, there were many days I surrendered to my sadness, when I was angry about the triggers that came out of nowhere, angry with my ex, angry with myself, and sometimes even angry with God. I would get headaches from the spiritual battle raging and often turned to Netflix, salty snacks, or a glass of wine to relieve the pain. I had many honest conversations with God, begging Him to reveal the purpose for the pain and for Him to show me how He was working in my life.

Slowly I began to recognize the days when I cried less, when I didn't get triggered, when I smiled, when I laughed, and when I accepted a compliment. These moments came slowly and might have even passed me by if I hadn't asked God to reveal them to me. I started writing these moments down so I wouldn't forget. I felt silly at first, but when sadness crept in so easily, I needed somewhere to go to help remind me of what God was doing for me.

"He who began a good work in you will carry it on to completion until the day of Christ Jesus" (Phil. 1:6 NIV).

I refuse to let divorce be the end of my story, and I have stopped letting the past define me. I am still learning the process of forgiveness—how to be grateful regardless of my circumstances and how to surrender, trust, and accept God's will for my life. So I continue to move forward.

Some days I tiptoe, still trying to be in control. Some days I walk confidently. But each day I embrace my most important label: a new creation in Christ.

Amelia S.

My husband helped me unload a car full of groceries on a Saturday morning; then he handed me divorce papers.

After twenty-five years of marriage, he was done. So much effort in marital therapy, pastoral counseling, accountability groups—all to end here?

Crushing fear and nausea fell at the same time. I ran to the bathroom, looked into the mirror, and said, "See, I told you this would happen."

I felt angry, afraid, worthless, and yet somehow not totally surprised. I had engaged a female Christian counselor a few months prior to this day because I, quite frankly, thought I was losing my mind.

Years of trying to keep up appearances of a healthy marriage had taken its toll on my sanity. I had wallpapered the walls of my mind with peaceful scenes of marital bliss while battling insecurities and cycling through unhealthy relational habits with my husband.

I'd spent twenty-five years being a devoted wife, raising three children, and building a home, yet he was walking away. At forty-six, I now faced my greatest fear: being alone and unloved.

How did this happen? I felt like I had "checked all the right boxes" in my Christian life. Didn't that count for anything?

I felt confused in my walk with the Lord, desperate for answers, for some rhythm of clarity and peace.

Suddenly our "friends" did not know quite what to do with me; I found myself excluded from familiar social and church gatherings. I felt resentment and unforgiveness because of the failure and shame of my crumbling marital facade.

About that time, I heard a Bible teaching about the gift of desperation. What? How could desperation be a gift? It felt more like a cruel joke, a nightmare I woke up to … Every. Single. Day.

As I walked through the stages of grief with my counselor, I began to see that the death of my marriage had been a slow, downhill spiral caused by years of unattended deep emotional issues. Our marriage was a grief unobserved. Activity had replaced intimacy. In truth, we had both lost our way.

Many Scriptures became so precious to me, but one was my bedrock for healing:

> Search me, O God, and know my heart!
>> Try me and know my thoughts!
> And see if there be any grievous way in me,
>> and lead me in the way everlasting! (Ps. 139:23–24 ESV)

Ouch! How sweetly chastening is God's Word! As I poured over these two verses, studying them, asking the Lord to reveal in me any "grievous ways," I became keenly aware of my dire need for Jesus to rescue me from myself. Desperation was indeed my gift.

I began to crave intimacy with Jesus more than anything else. On one particular day, as our divorce was about to be finalized, I faced the three-headed dragon: my legal issues, financial ruin, and the loss of longtime friendships. I whimpered through clenched teeth, "Rescue me, Lord."

The voice wasn't audible, but I heard it. My Savior said, "[Cast] *all* your anxieties on him, because he cares for you" (1 Pet. 5:7 ESV).

God cares for *me*. I released *all* my anxieties to the Lord. Peace washed over me. I felt hope for the first time in not just months but years. Slowly, I began to look forward to getting up each day and spending time in God's Word, knowing He would meet me there.

> *God cares for me. I released all my anxieties to the Lord.*

I realized that being single and divorced did not separate me from Jesus! More than merely accepting singleness, I became excited that a single life opened new doors. I interacted more deeply with my grown children. I helped build a house with Habitat for Humanity. During the summer, I tutored struggling students. All these activities I had yearned to do … I now had the gift of time.

The circumstances of my divorce and singleness led me to sweet communion with my Savior. My healing journey has led me down the path of God's all-sufficient grace and His steadfast love for me. What an amazing adventure!

Journaling Prompts

In what ways did you connect with these stories?

In your past?

In your current situation?

What would you like to apply moving forward?

Your Quiet Time

Moving Forward

> Take control of your life, and start living it instead of just surviving it.

Prepare

Prepare your heart for the study by memorizing this verse:

> For everything there is a season,
>   a time for every activity under heaven. (Eccl. 3:1)

Purge, Reflect, and Protect

1. During this painful season, have you been keeping a list of all the things you've lost as a result of your marriage? If so, capture those thoughts and submit them to God so seeds of bitterness and resentment don't block the Holy Spirit's power in your life.

2. Whatever you're feeling about your current state of singleness, remember this is just a season God is allowing you to walk through, and remember it is a gift from God because it allows His presence alone to consume and heal you. How can you view this season of life, even if unwanted or unexpected, as a blessing?

3. How can you discover new artistic talents or pick up old hobbies again?

4. What steps do you need to take to feel more like an empowered and independent woman?

5. What goals do you have for this season of singleness? How can you accomplish these?

Journaling Prompts

Today I feel …

But God's Word says …

Happiness Prompters, Healing Steps, and Caring for You Reminders

Read through the calls to action in *Living Unbroken* (see pages 118–19), and try to complete each of them before the next session.

Reading Assignment

Chapter 6: Breaking the Power of Shame

Chapter 7: Releasing the Burden of Guilt

Chapter 8: Girl, You Are Not Crazy

Reflections from the Group

Session Five

Chapters 6, 7, and 8

Chapter 6

Breaking the Power of Shame

Hope to Keep You Hanging On

Carol Ann F.

Oh God, please help me, I prayed. *I don't want to die!*

My husband had been sitting at the table using a knife to construct his green, hobby-store army figurines. I was attempting to resolve an argument when suddenly he jumped up from his chair, grabbed me, and held the sharp knife to my throat.

I had met him when I was eighteen, through a Christian friend. Initially I was attracted to his playful, gentle nature, but mostly I was attracted to his nonconformist philosophy on life. I had spent my childhood being forced to conform to the legalistic Italian-Catholic culture in which my mom had been raised.

My parents eventually went through an ugly divorce, and a few years later my siblings and I were living with my father. I had to hold the role of mom and take care of my siblings, all while still in high school. As a result, I began feeling resentful toward them and struggled to do all the things a mom should be doing. It was in the middle of this situation when I met my future husband, and we were soon married. I was only eighteen; he was twenty-six.

Over time, my husband began to isolate himself for hours, putting together his little green army figurines. I enrolled in college to study teaching and got a job at the campus library; he also got a job on campus as a cleaner. We started fighting more, and then he contracted adult measles, which only compounded our issues.

While he was sick, he only seemed to want his dad to read the Bible to him and his mom to cook for him. More and more I felt he had not married me but his mother, and he wanted me to do whatever his mother said even if I disagreed with her. This caused his frustration and anger with me to steadily grow worse, until one day, without warning, it turned physical.

I stood frozen, too scared to move or even breathe, as he pressed the knife against my throat. My thoughts were running as fast as my heart. *Is he going to slit my throat? Am I going to meet Christ?* But, suddenly, he put down the knife and let me go. I have no idea why. I only know who saved me from death in that moment—Jesus Christ.

> As a Christian, I felt incredibly sad and ashamed over the divorce, although I was extremely grateful to Christ to still be alive.

After this abusive event, I immediately left, and we divorced soon after. As a Christian, I felt incredibly sad and ashamed over the divorce, although I was extremely grateful to Christ to still be alive. Now, thirty years later, I can recall many times that Christ has saved me, including from a second abusive marriage. Psalm 32:7 became my mantra, which says, "You are my hiding place; you will protect me from trouble and surround me with songs of deliverance" (NIV).

My journey toward healing has been one of self-discovery. I was diagnosed with autism and ADHD at age fifty and more recently realized I am a codependent relationship addict. I started attending Celebrate Recovery meetings via Zoom, where I have a new Christian "forever family" and am learning it is Christ who defines me, not my addiction. I am also part of an extensive, supportive church family where I now live, and they have greatly helped me in my healing journey. God is good!

Regina L.

The click of the door lock echoed throughout the cold apartment. His footsteps grew more distant as he made his final descent away from the chaos that had ruled our household over the last year. Left behind were my child and me, a poignant visual reminder of my indiscretion. My husband had had enough. Enough of my immature ways, my inept attempts to hide my deception, enough of not living out our marriage vows and being the wife he wanted. Enough of me not saying, "I'm sorry."

The sound of the door closing behind him one final time signaled the end of a promising life I had carelessly let slip through my fingers. I had held so much hope at the beginning of our marriage. Hope that marriage would erase all the not-so-great childhood memories I desperately wanted to escape. Hope that my husband would help me forget the past and start over, fresh and new, free of the baggage I had carried for so long. I expected to gain so much from our marriage, but I put in little effort.

I was proud to hold the title of "wife," but I had little knowledge of what that looked like and no interest in doing the work it required. In short, sin reigned supreme. The foundation on which our union was based could be described as shaky at best. The exchange of marriage vows simply represented freedom from my past and not a commitment to our future. It's no wonder my eye wandered, followed shortly by the surrender of my entire body into the arms of someone who was not my husband, a temporary illicit escape from life that resulted in the birth of my child. I'd like to tell you I immediately owned my mess, but that wouldn't be true. I blamed my ex-husband for all our troubles—if only he had (insert pretty much anything), I wouldn't have had an affair. Oh my. Hope might have seemed out of reach, but one look at Scripture tells us "nothing is impossible with God" (Luke 1:37 TPT).

> *I'd like to tell you I immediately owned my mess, but that wouldn't be true.*

We can also find other lost souls, like Gomer, Hosea's wife. Their relationship, detailed in the book of Hosea, was filled with enough drama for their own present-day reality show: the breaking of the marriage covenant when Gomer strayed, the divorce that followed and Gomer's being sent away, the birth of one of her children and the questionable parentage. Their marriage was a mirror image of what was going on in the culture at the time: Israel's people had broken their vows to God by worshipping false gods. And the result? God was brokenhearted. But hope was not lost, because God's penchant for forgiveness led Hosea to welcome his wife back even though she had been unfaithful.

Through God, sins were forgiven and relationships restored.

Scripture clearly indicates that God will not allow us to stray from Him without consequences, just like the plight of the Israelites. My betrayal resulted in broken relationships that to this day require lots of work to navigate. Some of them may never be restored. God's commitment to those who love and honor Him is unfailing. While a happy reunion may not be a part of His plan, we can be confident of a promising future in His kingdom.

Since my divorce, I have recommitted my life to Christ and dealt with past demons that prevented me from loving unselfishly. The road to redemption has been filled with its fair share of challenges—that's for sure. Whispers of my indiscretions still find their way from people's lips all these years later, and forgiveness remains elusive for many. Spending time with my Father, my ministry coworkers, and my church family gives me the strength to carry on. To ignore the gossip. To allow forgiveness of myself and others. To love others as He loves me—unconditionally.

Journaling Prompts

In what ways did you connect with these stories?

In your past?

In your current situation?

What would you like to apply moving forward?

Your Quiet Time

Moving Forward

> Feelings of failure and embarrassment can be a tool the enemy uses to keep us suffering in silence. The best weight we can ever lose is the weight of other people's opinions.

Prepare

Prepare your heart for the study by memorizing this verse:

Now there is no condemnation for those who belong to Christ Jesus. (Rom. 8:1)

Watch the Session 5 Video

The video is available at **DavidCCook.org/access**, with access code **LivingUnbroken**.

Purge, Reflect, and Protect

1. Is the fear of others' opinions of you keeping you from getting out and socializing? Talk to God about it. Spend time investing in relationship with Him, and trust He'll take care of your reputation with others.

2. How can you move from shame to acceptance? What do you need to let go of?

3. Which healing step do you most need to complete? Why?

4. Reflect on what I shared on my blog more than a year after my separation occurred (see pages 127–28 in *Living Unbroken*). What do you need to be open about? What's holding you back? How might sharing help open the door for God to do new things in your heart, mind, and life?

Journaling Prompts

Today I feel …

But God's Word says …

Happiness Prompters, Healing Steps, and Caring for You Reminders

Read through the calls to action in *Living Unbroken* (see pages 132–33), and try to complete each of them before the next session.

Reflections from the Group

Chapter 7

Releasing the Burden of Guilt

Hope to Keep You Hanging On

Angela A.

We had it all. We were young, in love, and excited about spending the rest of our lives together. With an all-inclusive fairy-tale wedding, any onlooker would have agreed that we were the perfect couple and this marriage was a match made in heaven. No one could have convinced me that my beautiful marriage would one day end in an ugly divorce.

After we were married, it only took one month for the physical and emotional abuse to begin. Did I see the signs before I said "I do"? If I am being honest—yes, I saw the signs. However, I justified his behavior and rationalized that my unconditional love for him would somehow change his ways. Instead of heeding the red flags that God was persistently waving in front of me, I persuaded myself that marrying this man was God's plan for my life. I placed one foot in front of the other and walked down the aisle to one of the biggest mistakes of my life.

As the marriage continued, I allowed the occasional apologies and kind gestures to overshadow the consistent abusive patterns. I kept telling myself that if I tried harder, things would get better. When things started getting worse, I blamed myself for not trying hard enough. This approach sent me on a downward spiral to a bottomless pit of depression and despair. I felt like I was being punished. I questioned if God was even there. I put up a facade for my friends and family. I didn't want to let on that my marriage was failing … that I was a failure.

What made matters worse for me was that I married a pastor who was well known and loved by the members of the congregation. No one would ever believe what was happening to me behind closed doors.

I had nowhere to turn.

I had always dreamed of marrying a loving husband who respected and cared for me, a family man who was the head of the home and loved me like Christ loved the church, someone who would one day raise our children into a life of Christianity and focus his efforts on leading and nurturing our family. All of my dreams were shattered.

> *No one would ever believe what was happening to me behind closed doors. I had nowhere to turn.*

There was no loving husband, there were no children, and this was not a healthy Christian marriage. I felt like I was trapped in a recurring nightmare and there was no way to escape. I wanted out, but divorce would be such an embarrassing, public, sinful act. For the first time in my life, thoughts of suicide crept into my mind. It seemed to be the only viable solution, but I just couldn't bring myself to do that. I was so confused. I was always told that God hates divorce. I often wondered if He would also hate me if I got divorced.

On the contrary, God showed me just how much He loved me and cared for me. As I drew closer to Him in my weakest moment, I came to know Him as my strong tower (see Prov. 18:10 NASB). God provided a close friend who fasted and prayed for me through this ordeal. I mustered up the courage to leave my husband, move in with my friend and her family, and file for divorce. I truly believed that God was full of mercy and grace, which helped me push past feelings of fear, shame, and guilt. I knew He would give me another chance, restore what was lost, and I would one day be married and have a family of my dreams.

Two years later, that day came. I met and eventually married a man who was exactly what I'd prayed for. We also have two children, which is a fulfillment of God's promise to me. When I look back over my life and recollect where I have been, I am reminded that God is faithful! He gave me "beauty instead of ashes, the oil of joy instead of mourning, and a garment of praise instead of a spirit of despair" (Isa. 61:3 NIV).

God took my life that was once broken, and He made it whole. My family is a living testimony that God restores, and for this reason, I will be forever grateful to Him.

Kristin G.

My marriage was difficult. But I didn't think it was *divorce-level* difficult. My life was a complete mess, but I didn't realize how deep I was in the pit of despair. The first mention of separation came in July of 2018. That conversation blindsided me like nothing else ever had. The next two nights were spent on the couch because I couldn't sleep. In the middle of the second night, God showed up. I was praying, crying out to Him to change me. To help me. To show me how I had gotten here. And like a movie playing before my eyes, God showed me what I needed to know.

A traumatic event never dealt with, unforgiveness, and sin weighed me down like a two-hundred-pound weight. The stripping of pride, forgiveness, confession, and repentance lifted that two-hundred-pound weight off. In the dawn of a new day, I felt like a new person. My eyes were opened, the depression was gone, and I knew God had miraculously redeemed me. In James 4:10, it says, "Humble yourselves in the presence of the Lord, and He will exalt you" (NASB).

What I did not know at the time was that God was preparing me for the most difficult journey of my life. When my husband did finally leave in January of 2019, I knew that the only way to survive was to draw close to the Lord. I made the decision to honor God above all else *and* to honor and respect my husband, no matter what. Those two decisions protected me from making mistakes. I needed my two young-adult daughters to see their mom walking a very difficult path, trusting the Lord with every step.

The journey has been long and difficult. Love needs trust and honesty to survive. What I didn't have in my marriage, I now needed to learn how to do on my own. And that was to trust God and believe that what He says is true.

I clearly remember the day I finally accepted divorce was inevitable and committed to believe God would be by my side, no matter what. Through a river of tears I said out loud, "I trust You, Lord." He was already taking care of me, but I needed to let go of what I wanted and place it at the feet of Jesus, trusting that He would continue to take care of me.

> I'd never kept a journal, but I knew I wanted to record all the ways God was showing up on this journey.

Staying close to the Lord by immersing myself in my Bible, listening to praise and worship music, listening to Christian podcasts, and meeting daily with God in prayer kept me grounded on this journey. There were days I begged God to take me home just so I could be relieved of the pain. His encouragement and provision always came at just the right time.

My counselor suggested I start writing in a journal. I'd never kept a journal, but I knew I wanted to record all the ways God was showing up on this journey. His faithfulness to me throughout this entire process has been nothing short of amazing and miraculous. Every time God showed up, I wrote it down. What I have now are pages and pages of how God has provided for me daily. He has made me confident to make decisions and able to understand things. Friends who, without hesitation, walked this path with me have included neighbors who showed up, family members who supported me, a church family that helped me, a Bible study group that prayed without ceasing, and strangers who offered words of encouragement.

My journal entries have become a collection of answered prayers, His provision, His perfect timing, His help, and His love. These journals are my testimony of faith.

Journaling Prompts

In what ways did you connect with these stories?

In your past?

In your current situation?

What would you like to apply moving forward?

Your Quiet Time

Moving Forward

> He is never too far away to hear our cries for rescue,
> and we are never too far from His grace to be forgiven.

Prepare

Prepare your heart for the study by memorizing this verse:

> He has removed our sins as far from us
>   as the east is from the west. (Ps. 103:12)

Purge, Reflect, and Protect

1. Are regrets about the past burdening your heart with guilt? God already knows everything you've ever done or will do, so there's no need to prolong your misery. Write a letter of repentance asking God to remove the guilt you feel and give you peace.

2. What skeletons do you need to drag out of your closet? How can you begin healing?

3. Read the two quotes below (from pages 136 and 149 in *Living Unbroken*), and reflect on their meaning. How do these quotes give you hope, comfort, or freedom from something that has been holding your heart hostage?

    Guilt is to the soul what pain is to the body.

    He is never too far away to hear our cries for rescue, and we are never too far from His grace to be forgiven.

4. Reflect on Ephesians 6:10–18 (MSG). Which words resonate with you the most?

Journaling Prompts

Today I feel …

But God's Word says …

Happiness Prompters, Healing Steps, and Caring for You Reminders

Read through the calls to action in *Living Unbroken* (see pages 150–53), and try to complete each of them before the next session.

Reflections from the Group

Chapter 8

Girl, You Are Not Crazy

Hope to Keep You Hanging On

Sandy N.

My husband of twenty-four years got involved with a much younger coworker who was also married, and despite my best efforts, prayers, and fasting, he would not come to his senses. Both marriages ended, they married each other, and my journey of walking through the valley of the shadow of death began.

Up until this happening, I had had, for the most part, a sweet and good life. I loved my now ex-husband deeply and was happy with our beautiful family and life. Unlike a lot of couples, we had been happily married throughout most of the marriage. Of all the things I'd feared in life, losing my husband to an affair and subsequent divorce was something I simply never dreamed would happen.

Yet it did, and I found myself in that valley. But I learned that the valley is just a place that we are walking "through." A valley is never meant to be a place we stay! Notice God's choice of words in Psalm 23:4: "Even though I walk through the darkest valley." *Through.* Not a place to camp but a place we are only passing through. It may seem like the darkest pit from which there is no escape, but it is also a place where we do not have to be filled with fear. Consider the rest of the verse: "I will not be afraid, for you are close beside me. Your rod and your staff protect and comfort me." He is with us in those dark times so we need not fear, and He promises to never leave our side and to tend to our hurting hearts.

What a powerhouse of promises in one little Scripture! Not only does God promise to be with us in this place of suffering, He promises there is an end to the journey through the valley. What comfort we can have in knowing this.

When my life got turned upside down, I did the only thing I knew to do as a believer— run to the arms of God. God first comforted me with His rod and staff … His precious Word. He began immediately giving me Scripture for each season to steady me and to give me something to cling to.

In my unimaginable pain, I sought Him like I never had in my life. I had no choice but to trust Him. I immediately began feeling His presence so strongly and, every day, asking Him to show me the way. He guided, strengthened, counseled, comforted, and provided for me. I wish I could tell you all the ways! But even though I knew He was right there with me, I still struggled so deeply that I had times when I just simply did not think I could live.

> *I was in a position for the first time in my life where I had no choice but to trust Him completely for everything.*

One of the very hardest parts of all for me was the why. *Why on earth, Lord?* I tried to take the advice of Christian friends who told me I just had to take this on faith and that I probably wouldn't have those answers this side of heaven. Although I tried to accept that precept, I simply couldn't. I just knew there was no way God had allowed this to happen to me for no reason, or that I should just accept this from His hand and move on. I knew intuitively there had to be greater purpose in this.

Being a faithful God, He gradually gave me insight into the why. A couple of years into my journey, He showed me my marriage had actually been an "Egypt." With rose-colored glasses on, I had been unable to see the truth of my marriage for many years. My ex-husband and I were unequally yoked, but I didn't realize it at the time.

The finalization of my divorce was the beginning of a wilderness experience for me, much like the Israelites. I was in a position for the first time in my life where I had no choice but to trust Him completely for everything. He sent manna from heaven every day! It was truly amazing. I soon came to realize that during this season He was teaching me to trust Him daily for everything my children and I needed. But even so, I still struggled most every day in some way. My grief was deep and the psychological effects were crazy-making.

One morning, during a sweet time of fellowship with Him, I was thinking back over all that had happened, how much my faith had grown, and how God had seen us through. But this time, I heard Him say something else in my spirit: *"to prove your faith was genuine."* I knew it was a Scripture and quickly looked it up. First Peter 1:7 says, "These have come so that the *proven genuineness of your faith …*" (NIV).

Wow. There it was. And then He gave me this verse too: "Remember how the LORD your God led you all the way in the wilderness these forty years, *to humble and test you in order to know what was in your heart,* whether or not you would keep his commands" (Deut. 8:2 NIV).

God opened my eyes to see that what had happened to me could be summed up in these two verses … to prove my faith was genuine, to humble me, to test me, and to see if I would keep His commands. There was purpose in all this heartache. He was in control the whole time! He was truly my Unfailing Love.

I believe now that I'm out of the wilderness and entering my Promised Land. Where the milk and honey are flowing. Where it was worth everything I went through to get there.

Melissa W.

Begging the Lord to bring me home to heaven had become my fight song. But this particular morning, my eyes flew wide open after months of living in a semiconscious coma brought on by physical and psychological abuse. God's Holy Spirit impressed upon my spirit to "wake up!"

A mirror hadn't been a part of my life for a good four months. A shower hadn't been part of my life in at least five weeks, much less brushing my teeth or hair. I'd put on sixty pounds. And now, as I faced it, the mirror revealed a stranger who looked utterly shattered and horrified at the damage done to her body from the night before and the months leading up to it. Barely recognizable. I stared at this dead woman and wept.

Addictions and depression on both sides had led up to the demise of my marriage. I lived in a constant state of condemnation for the terrible choices I'd made. Suddenly I found myself awake, and God imparted clarity on what to do next.

Getting the police involved and a two-year protection order paved the way for other life-altering transformations. Not long after this incident, I moved out of state to a Christian women's recovery home, where I didn't have a phone, TV, or internet access for a full year. A lawyer for abused women helped me get a divorce for free through the mail.

At this home I startled easily and stayed in constant fight-or-flight mode whenever people were arguing or just having fun. In church services, when pastors delivered "passionate" messages that sounded a lot like yelling to me, memories of the abuse would flood in like a tsunami. I sobbed silently in the pew, unable to control my mind or body.

God's solution to these PTSD symptoms was His Word. Alive. Mighty. Exquisite. Always healing. Always working. Always the answer! I asked the Lord to give me a verse to help me through these painful and embarrassing reactions. After a while in prayer, He impressed upon my heart John 14:18, which says, "I will not leave you comfortless: I will come to you" (KJV). This verse proved short enough to recall easily, and a refreshing awareness of His presence and promises flowed through me like a roaring waterfall while I meditated on these words.

> God's solution to these PTSD symptoms was His Word. Alive. Mighty. Exquisite. Always healing. Always working. Always the answer!

Whenever I felt caught off guard, I discovered a new freedom and victory in our True Comforter—His Holy Spirit. By looking up the definitions to the word *comfort* in the Webster 1828 dictionary, I saw precious and personal meanings that greeted me like a warm hug. *Comfort* can mean "relief from pain" and "relief from distress of mind."*

Over time, repeating this verse in my mind made the PTSD symptoms diminish. When a trigger tempts my mind now, Jesus reminds me to lean into the supernatural power of His Word and to hold on to Him as my anchor of comfort.

Be encouraged, and ask God to restore your spirit and give you a verse for this season of your life. It will become deeply personal and healing. Swimming in Psalms for comfort is an amazing remedy for a mind in distress. I believe He longs to do a wonder in you too, and He will cover you with comfort to help you get through.

---

* Noah Webster, *An American Dictionary of the English Language*, vol. 1 (New York: S. Converse, 1828), s.v. "comfort."

Journaling Prompts

In what ways did you connect with these stories?

In your past?

In your current situation?

What would you like to apply moving forward?

Your Quiet Time

Moving Forward

> *Girl, you are not crazy, and you are not incapable of moving forward and living a happy, joy-filled life.*

Prepare

Prepare your heart for the study by memorizing this verse:

> Those who trust in the LORD will find new strength.
>
> > They will soar high on wings like eagles.
>
> They will run and not grow weary.
>
> > They will walk and not faint. (Isa. 40:31)

Purge, Reflect, and Protect

1. How confident are you about the future? Do you believe God still has a plan for you that's good, despite the hardships in your life right now? Empty your mind onto the space below, and talk through with Jesus any obstacles you see.

2. Are you relieved to know you aren't crazy for feeling or struggling in the ways you do? How does recognizing this help you feel a little better about how you're coping with your situation?

3. Reflect on these words: "With great trauma comes great stress." What are you currently stressed about? What parts of PTSD are you struggling with, if any?

4. Has it been helpful to discover your triggers? How will you move forward and not let others steal your future happiness?

Journaling Prompts

Today I feel …

But God's Word says …

Happiness Prompters, Healing Steps, and Caring for You Reminders

Read through the calls to action in *Living Unbroken* (see pages 172–74), and try to complete each of them before the next session.

Reading Assignment

Chapter 9: Love Conquers All

Chapter 10: It's Time to Turn the Page

Reflections from the Group

Session Six

Chapters 9 and 10

Love Conquers All

Hope to Keep You Hanging On

Lisa F.

The raindrops sliding down my windshield were a welcome cover for the waterfall cascading down my cheeks. I sat in the grocery store parking lot and let my heart break open, my world shattering down around me as my thoughts echoed *I'm going to get divorced*. I wasn't to learn the full ramifications of that reality until later, but what I did know in that instant was that two of the most precious and beautiful hearts were about to be ripped apart.

At five and almost two years old, my kids were looking at a lifetime of wounds, pain, acting out, instability, brokenness, and questioning love itself. We were now going to be a statistic. A label. They were going to have gaps—chasms in their innocence I couldn't cover. All because one man couldn't honor his marriage vows to forsake all others. The breaks and wounds he suffered in his childhood would now be echoed in *my* children's lives. That was their legacy, and I could see their future as clearly as the rain-soaked window I sat crumpled against.

I was out of tears, breath, and willpower—until suddenly I was interrupted. *"Do you trust Me to bridge the gap for your kids?"* I felt startled and looked to my right. I knew I hadn't audibly heard a voice, and yet … had I? I then realized Jesus was in my van with me. I heard it again. *"Do you trust Me to bridge the gap for your kids?"* As an unexpected, overwhelming peace settled into my chest, I knew … yes … yes, I could.

I wish I could tell you the road ahead of me became easy. That I didn't lie awake on my bedroom floor some nights crying so hard my whole body hurt and then forcing myself to breathe afterward. I also wish I could tell you that navigating a divorce with someone clinically diagnosed with a personality disorder became simple. Both his therapist and mine had tough sessions where they outlined the likely years-long, painful process I would be facing. Lawyers encouraged me to fight hard for full custody and the works. But deep down inside I could hear God speaking very firmly to me: "The LORD will fight for you; you need only to be still" (Ex. 14:14 NIV).

I spent a lot of time in prayer over that verse. Obedience to the voice I knew to be God's went against the advice of a lot of professionals. But throughout this ordeal, Jesus had never left my side. He held me while I cried, and I could feel Him grieving with me. He would sing me to sleep and promised someday I would smile again. And this same Jesus, who had sat in my van asking me to trust Him with my kids, was quite directly telling me to stop fighting for them and let Him fight for them instead. So I did.

> *It has been okay, only because God said it would be and because He continues to fight on my behalf.*

I stood down, elected not to retain any of the lawyers I'd interviewed, and dove headlong into the presence of God. And I stayed there. Then one day, three months later, everything changed. My then-husband was meeting with me at a local restaurant to try to finalize the details of our custody agreement. Until that point, he had vehemently opposed anything I asked for, no matter how it might affect the kids. We picked a public place for this discussion because I was afraid to be alone with him.

As we sat in that booth, passing the anger baton back and forth, I could see him spiraling. When he was finally unable to control his volume and we began receiving concerned looks from other restaurant guests, he walked out. I slumped back in the booth in defeat, completely exhausted, letting out a deep sigh as I looked up and glanced out the restaurant window to see he had made it as far as the block retaining wall surrounding a sidewalk planter. He'd slumped down on the ledge and was just sitting there, head hanging down in the same defeat that was drowning me. I heard the Lord say, *"Go sit next to him."*

I did *not* want to go sit next to the man who moments earlier had been spitting venomous slander in my face. But I chose to obey. I walked outside and slowly sat down next to him on that block wall. I leaned against his arm and just sat there in silence, staring at the ground. And he broke. Friend, I watched as God took the heart of that man next to me and turned it a full 180 degrees. His face changed, light came back into his eyes, his shoulders straightened, and hope returned. Within the hour, we'd completely rewritten the entire custody agreement. It was and still is a thing of beauty.

The divorce was finalized a mere two months later with no judges involved. Hebrews 10:23 says, "So now wrap your heart tightly around the hope that lives within us, knowing that God always keeps his promises" (TPT). I think it's easy to read that verse and celebrate the light and fluffy part where God keeps His promises, but that's not where hope lives. Hope lives in the deep darkness where all those promises seem to evaporate before our very eyes. It is in that moment we get to choose whether we look at the storm or at His face.

Jesus told me that rainy day that He would cover my kids. If I could trust Him, it would be okay. So I chose to trust Him. More than once and often. It's been challenging, and my kids are still young, so it's not over yet, but guess what? It has been okay, only because God said it would be and because He continues to fight on my behalf.

Jennifer C.

"Tell me how you're doing," she said. Not even an actual question. Just a statement that asked a lot, given all that was happening in our family's life.

She always asked questions. That was her job. She was a part of the process—this awful divorce process—that required many voices helping to figure out life for our family across two households now that divorce was our reality. I was accustomed to her questions about how the kids were doing. But … one about me was unexpected.

Less than a year earlier, life had changed dramatically for our family. I'd spent the months since navigating a difficult, exhausting legal process and adapting to single-parent life. Her comment caught me off guard, and in an instant I was sobbing.

As she brought the box of Kleenex to the table, all I could say was, "This is not the example I wanted to give my children."

My parents had been married more than forty years at that point, and my maternal grandparents for sixty-five. I grew up with a front row seat to two marriages that lasted. Not perfect marriages by any means. But real ones that showed what it was like to make it through the valleys in life with relationships intact. These awful recent months had brought into full view the fact that I was unable to do what they had done.

I wasn't going to give my children an example of how marriage can last. And that realization was devastating.

The gentle observation shared back to me is one I will never forget.

"You *are* giving them an example. You're showing them what to do—and how to survive—when things don't go the way you hoped."

When I became a mom, the instruction from Proverbs 22:6 to train my children for how they should live was always on my mind: "Train up a child in the way he should go: and when he is old, he will not depart from it" (KJV). I thought that meant teaching them to be kind, polite, and aware of God as their Maker and Jesus as their Savior.

The naivete that comes with being a new parent often blinds us to the reality that parenting also includes teaching children how to keep their eyes on God when life goes in directions we wouldn't choose. When people make decisions that disappoint, hurt, and sometimes leave us with only less-than-ideal next steps.

As much as we'd love to prevent it, our children will experience disappointment, people will hurt their hearts, and at some point they will find themselves with no good options forward. A crucial part of our job is to train them for the inevitable.

> We have the chance every day, especially in those hard, dark seasons, to show our children that God is just as much with them in the dark as He is on their best days.

So when they look back with the context that only age and maturity can bring, what will our children remember from watching us navigate this hard road?

My prayer for my children—and yours—is that they will see that God is always the same, even when we find ourselves on a journey that feels far from Him. When reality hits and divorce enters our personal experience, it can feel like we have wandered alone into a dark place where surely the Lord will never be.

But God promises His people that He never leaves us—even in our greatest disappointments and failures. He is the God of dark places and heartbreaking realities. He is the God of this fallen world, and there is no place too deep, dark, or isolated for Him to go (see Josh. 1:9).

When our children inevitably face their own disappointment or heartache, remember they've been watching us encounter the roughness of this broken world. We have the chance every day, especially in those hard, dark seasons, to show them that God is just as much with them in the dark as He is on their best days.

Even when the example is one you never would choose to give your children, God will use it—and you, my friend—to prepare them for their own walk through the hard edges of life.

Journaling Prompts

In what ways did you connect with these stories?

In your past?

In your current situation?

What would you like to apply moving forward?

Your Quiet Time

Moving Forward

God doesn't expect perfection from you, so don't expect it from yourself.

Prepare

Prepare your heart for the study by memorizing this verse:

> We know how much God loves us, and we have put our trust in his love. God is love, and all who live in love live in God, and God lives in them. (1 John 4:16)

Watch the Session 6 Video

The video is available at **DavidCCook.org/access**, with access code **LivingUnbroken**.

Purge, Reflect, and Protect

1. Are you questioning your value and lovability as a result of your divorce? Spend time in prayer asking Jesus to heal the wounds left behind so you can love others and God the way He loves you.

2. How does it make you feel to love on others, and what benefits do you derive from it on a personal level? What could you do for yourself, your children, or others that would show extra love?

3. Which promises of God resonate with you? Why?

4. Reflect on these words: "Divorce doesn't label us as broken. It labels us as human." How can you begin to love yourself and see yourself as unbroken, whole, and valuable? What lies do you need to stop believing?

Journaling Prompts

Today I feel …

But God's Word says …

Happiness Prompters, Healing Steps, and Caring for You Reminders

Read through the calls to action in *Living Unbroken* (see pages 189–90), and try to complete each of them before the next session.

Reflections from the Group

Chapter 10

It's Time to Turn the Page

Hope to Keep You Hanging On

Christine L.

Alcoholism and mental illness are the scariest things to have in a marriage. I was married for thirty-five years, and my husband was lost in both. I loved him so much, but as the years went by, I became sicker too—in an enabling pattern that I was unable to find a way out of, especially as he gradually became more unstable.

The day of the last straw, I realized I had to leave for my own safety. There was no other choice, and I was scared to death. I knew that God was going to take care of me, but at the same time I was filled with fear. Both of our grown sons agreed with me, and so did my sister. I had their support, but I did not feel any braver.

As I packed my things and drove to my sister's home, I was shaking and crying. All kinds of questions, doubt, and confusion ran through my mind. The one verse that God kept reminding me of as I prayed was Jeremiah 29:11–14: "'I know the plans I have for you,' says the LORD. 'They are plans for good and not for disaster, to give you a future and a hope. In those days when you pray, I will listen. If you look for me wholeheartedly, you will find me. I will be found by you,' says the LORD." I knew God's plans for me were to prosper and not to harm me but to give me a hope and a future. Still, I struggled to trust Him and to believe those truths.

Over the next few days, I watched as God answered my prayers and worked things out as only He can. A restraining order was granted; a Baker Act was put in place (something only God could do). A lawyer took my case and helped begin the divorce process, making it as painless as she could. My sons and sister rallied around me, and God spoke words of love and encouragement through them to pull me through each moment. Friends were praying, and I felt the power of prayer through each of them.

Each moment that fear would grip my heart again as I worried over bad things that might happen (but never did), God would whisper the verse to me again to remind me of what is true. Only God could have removed me from the toxic relationship and taken care of everything. I am still in awe of His amazing love and what an awesome God He is.

> Each moment that fear would grip my heart again as I worried over bad things that might happen (but never did), God would whisper the verse to me again to remind me of what is true.

Five years later, I am in a better place and continue to heal and grow in conquering my fears. The divorce was finalized. I had two years of Al-Anon and counseling at my church. I have made progress with my enabling and learned to set boundaries. My husband and I have no contact, for my safety and sanity. My sons have come to terms with their father and the divorce and are always supportive of me. My sister is still my rock and is always ready to listen.

I want to encourage you, sister. If you are filled with fear and afraid to walk away from a marriage that has addiction and mental illness, know that I got through it and you can too. Hang on tight to a verse that reminds you of what is true, stay focused in prayer, and take one step at a time. You can survive, and in time, you will begin to thrive.

I am praying for you, that you will be filled with His peace as you walk through this journey.

Meagan S.

At age twenty-one, I walked down the church aisle, stood up in front of one hundred people, and said, "I do." It was a simple, happy day. But the picture I had of happily-ever-after and growing old together was torn to shreds by the reality of a tumultuous marriage and a husband who looked for happiness with someone else.

A few days before my twenty-eighth birthday, I filed for divorce after realizing reconciliation wasn't possible. I was devastated. This wasn't the life I had planned or wanted. I never imagined becoming a single mom of two young girls, having to share them on holidays and spend time away from them each week, or living with the reality of my girls having another family without me. I dealt with grief, depression, anxiety for the future, and utter heartbreak. I thought I would never get beyond the hurt. But God showed me daily just how much He loved me and how He was walking through it with me.

When I felt unloved, I would open the mailbox to find cards and letters of encouragement. When my car unexpectedly broke down, generous friends anonymously gifted me a sum of money that enabled me to purchase a used car. When all I could do was cry, my family and friends sat with me and listened. A counselor offered me sessions free of charge. God opened the door for me to go back to working in my church office, which allowed me to spend more time with my girls. He showed me in more ways than I can describe how He was watching over me and taking care of me. I found the Psalms to be a huge comfort.

As I read about all the hardships and heartaches of the psalmists, I noticed how they continued to trust in God and be strengthened by Him. I especially enjoyed Psalm 73, which Asaph wrote about a time of turmoil in his own life when it felt like the wicked were prospering and would never face justice. In verse 26, he said, "My flesh and my heart may fail, but God is the strength of my heart and my portion forever" (ESV). This verse has become my favorite Bible verse because it encapsulates what I have learned through my divorce and in the four years since.

When I didn't even feel like I could get out of bed and face the day, God gave my heart strength. Though I lost the closest human relationship I had, I have grown so much closer to the Lord through my heartache. He's my portion—my inheritance through my faith in Christ—and that's an even better relationship.

He's the friend who's always there, always listens, and always loves me, no matter what. In Isaiah 54, He described Himself as Israel's husband. In the New Testament, the church is called the bride of Christ. As believers, we are in a deep, personally connected relationship—like the closeness of a marriage relationship—with God Himself. That brings me hope on the hard days and comforts me when I feel lonely.

> When I didn't even feel like I could get out of bed and face the day, God gave my heart strength.

If you have endured the pain of divorce or are going through it now, I encourage you to let God be the strength of your heart. He is your portion forever! According to Hebrews 13:5, He "will never leave you nor forsake you" (ESV). The preceding verse in that chapter talks about marriage and adultery, a circumstance involved in many divorces.

Though your spouse may have left you, God never will. Though your marriage may be over, you are loved beyond measure by the God who created you. He is the strength of your broken heart.

Journaling Prompts

In what ways did you connect with these stories?

In your past?

In your current situation?

What would you like to apply moving forward?

Your Quiet Time

Moving Forward

> Giving yourself permission to dream is a powerful way to propel yourself forward.

Prepare

Prepare your heart for the study by memorizing this verse:

> "I know the plans I have for you," says the LORD. "They are plans for good and not for disaster, to give you a future and a hope." (Jer. 29:11)

Purge, Reflect, and Protect

1. Is disappointment keeping you focused on the past? Find a quiet spot where you can be alone with God, and ask Him to reveal any unresolved anger or bitterness that may be creating a barrier to your healing.

2. Reflect on these words: "The only thing harder than letting go is holding on to what can't be." Do you agree with this statement? If so, what is it you need to let go of and accept?

3. How would letting go of what can't be or accepting what has happened help you step into the future with enthusiasm and optimism? Imagine how your life would change for the good!

Bonus Questions

1. Which tips from *Living Unbroken* do you want to try? Why?

2. How can you better yourself? What work do you need to do to embrace your "new"?

3. Do you believe God is doing something new in your heart and your life? How?

Journaling Prompts

Today I feel …

But God's Word says …

Happiness Prompters, Healing Steps, and Caring for You Reminders

Read through the calls to action in *Living Unbroken* (see pages 211–13), and try to complete each of them before the next session.

Reflections from the Group

Session Seven

Finishing Well

Embracing the New

Sweet friend, you did it! I know your healing journey has just begun, but hopefully this study has left you feeling more confident in yourself, your ability to take back control of your life, and your faith in your heavenly Father.

In this last gathering with your group, you'll listen to my concluding video and share your final thoughts with your fellow study members. Your group leader will also set aside time during this session for you to revisit your Heart Check table and record the rankings for your current thoughts and emotions. Hopefully you'll see great progress in many areas of your heart and mind. Although healing takes time, I pray each day will continue to get a little easier for you.

For your last Prepare activity, I want to encourage you to memorize Isaiah 43:19:

> I am about to do something new.
> See, I have already begun! Do you not see it?

In this passage of the Bible, Isaiah portrayed God as a holy Father who can be trusted with our present and our future. A God who keeps His promises to protect and provide and who empowers His people to live joyful, peace-filled lives.

> *As hard as it feels, try to let go of what isn't and instead embrace the new season God has you in right now.*

God is doing something new in your life and in your heart. As hard as it feels, try to let go of what isn't and instead embrace the new season God has you in right now.

When doubt, fear, or sorrow creep in occasionally, which will happen, turn back to God and recall Isaiah 43:19, repeating out loud, "I trust You, Lord, even with all this new. Help me see and feel You at work in me and my life."

From this day forward, let your heart be happy and keep your mind focused on a new, positive perspective about the future. God wants that for you, and you deserve it.

Tracie

Watch the Session 7 Video

The video is available at **DavidCCook.org/access**, with access code **LivingUnbroken**.

Reflections from the Group

Heart Check

Personal Growth and Healing Scale

Healing and growth during this difficult journey of separation and divorce is hard, but it is possible and it will happen! Nothing is more motivating than being able to see our progress, which serves as a visual reminder that God is at work in our hearts and our lives.

For each category below, rank **how you are feeling today on a scale of 1 to 10 (with 1 being the worst and 10 being the best)**. There is also space to add in your own topics or current struggles and challenges.

At the end of the study, come back to this table and assess yourself again to see just how far you have come and how much you have grown in heart, mind, and spirit!

God is at work in our hearts and our lives.

How do you currently feel about your ...	Beginning of Study	End of Study
Level of trust in God's plans		
Closeness and relationship with God		
Understanding of your identity and value in Jesus		
Confidence in God's promise to meet all your needs		
Belief in His unconditional love for you		
Belief in your value as a woman		
Belief in your worth as a child of God		
Hope for a joy-filled life despite your circumstances		
Ability to be a good mom		
Emotional well-being and the handling of your emotions		
Anger toward your ex-spouse		
Ability to forgive your ex-spouse and anyone else who hurt you		
Ability to forgive yourself for mistakes		
Feelings of shame about your divorce		
Feelings of shame about your ex-spouse's behaviors		
Feelings of guilt for the current situation and/or your own choices		
Belief that your actions are unforgivable by God or others		
Level of support from people in your church or community		
Level of support from family and close friends		
Ability to feel positive and hopeful about the future		
Body image and feelings of self-confidence		
Willingness to socialize and meet new people		
Ability to embrace this new season of life and make the best of it		

How do you currently feel about your ...	Beginning of Study	End of Study

Thirty-Three Journaling Prompts

1. "With God all things are possible" (Matt. 19:26 ESV). What does this verse mean to me?

2. An aspect of God's character He recently revealed to me is …

3. I feel God's presence most when …

4. My favorite Scripture passage is …

5. Right now, do I feel close to or far away from God? Why do I feel this way?

6. As I reflect on this day, where did I see God at work?

7. Three ways I'd like God to transform me are …

8. List all the things I believe about God, and pick one to praise Him for as I walk through this day.

9. In His perfect timing, God will …

10. This week I was most blessed by …

11. A step of obedience God is compelling me to take is …

12. An area where I need to put more trust in God is …

13. One lesson I learned from Scripture this week is …

14. If I were sitting across from Jesus and He looked me in the eye and said, "Tell Me what you need," how would I respond?

15. I feel most distant from God when …

16. List five things I'm truly grateful for and what makes them stand out in my mind.

17. Write down three things I can start doing today to draw closer to God.

18. Reflect on a time God answered my prayers (including all the details I can remember).

19. Is there a song that God has been using to speak to me recently? Incorporate lines from that song in a prayer of trust and surrender to God.

20. My enthusiasm for Jesus is increased when …

21. What situations in my life are triggers for anxious feelings? Write them down, and ask God to help me overcome these triggers.

22. Are there people, desires, or other things in my life that are obstacles to my healing and moving forward? Prayerfully turn these over to God, and write about how I can let go of, remove, or change these unhealthy patterns and/or relationships.

23. When was a time I strongly felt God's presence in my life? How did it make me feel? How can that experience infuse me with new hope every day?

24. What am I most worried about today? How would I feel if I fully surrendered these worries to God?

25. Sometimes I get angry with God about …

26. What am I learning about myself through this painful experience? How am I growing?

27. What have I accomplished that I didn't know I could do on my own? How did that make me feel?

28. Make a list of things that bring a smile to my face.

29. What are five activities I'd like to do more of? How can I make more time for them?

30. I could use more of …

31. I could use less of …

32. I know there are people who need encouragement as much as I do. List the names of these people. I will reach out to them and then come back and write about those new or restored connections.

33. Journaling has helped my faith by …

Acknowledgments

I am so thankful for so many people who have poured their hearts into me and the message of this book and wanted to take time to give them the recognition they deserve.

David C Cook Publishing has been a part of my life now for many years, and I can't imagine having a more wonderful publisher to work with. Thank you to Susan McPherson and Annette Brickbealer for their belief in my message, support of my ideas, willingness to be flexible when life gets in the way, and unmatched compassion and friendship.

Thank you to my agent, Greg Johnson with WordServe Literary Group, who has been my supporter for many years and is always willing to go to bat for me and help with whatever is needed.

My mom, Barbara, and my amazing children, Morgan, Kaitlyn, and Michael, who have been my support system and best friends through this difficult journey we have all been on. I am so blessed to have each one of them in my life and could not be where I am today without them by my side.

A precious team of women helped bring this workbook to life. They each felt called by God to volunteer their time, heart, and energy to brainstorm and harvest content that would help other women heal, recover, and find happiness and wholeness. I am so thankful for them.

Kelly Kirby Worley—thank you for your incredible heart and your passion to help women going through separation and divorce. I will be forever grateful for your willingness to invest your time, energy, and heart in this recovery program to help women heal. Your input and assistance were invaluable.

Thank you, Kellie Tuten, Rachel Sweatt, and Taylor Murray, for the time and effort you invested in this project, as well as for your friendship and support. It was a blessing getting to know each of you and working alongside you in your own writing journeys. I know God will bless your efforts and open doors for your words to get into the world.

Last, I want to express special, heartfelt gratitude to each of the women who were willing to vulnerably share the painful details of their separation and divorce journeys in this workbook, as well as the hope, restoration, and renewed joy God brought into their lives. These real-life stories are going to give countless women hope and help them embrace the truth that in time God will restore and renew their hearts and lives too. Thank you for allowing God to turn your pain into purpose.

More from Tracie Miles

*Living Unbroken: Reclaiming Your Life
and Your Heart after Divorce*

Love Life Again: Finding Joy When Life Is Hard

*Unsinkable Faith: God-Filled Strategies to
Transform the Way You Think, Feel, and Live*

*Stress Less Living: God-Centered Solutions
When You're Stretched Too Thin*

*Your Life Still Counts: How God Uses
Your Past to Create a Beautiful Future*

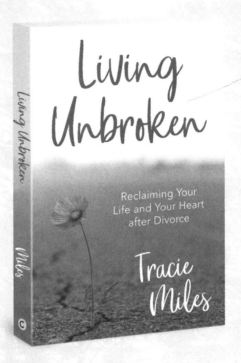

Your Marriage May Be Broken But You Don't Have to Be

In *Living Unbroken*, drawing from her own experience with divorce,
Tracie Miles addresses the heartbreak of loss that comes from the breakup
of a marriage while providing practical tips and guidance to women for
overcoming the belief they will never be happy again, dispelling the myth
that divorce can't be Christian, and teaching scriptural truths to help
women embrace renewed purpose and joy.

Available in print and digital
wherever books are sold

DAVID C COOK

transforming lives together